D1739957

Introducing Finger Painting

Introducing
Finger Painting

Guy Scott

B. T. Batsford Limited · London

©Guy Scott 1973

First published 1973
ISBN 0 7134 2432 X

Filmset by Filmtype Services Limited, Scarborough
Printed in Great Britain by Cox and Wyman Limited, Fakenham
for the publisher
B T Batsford Limited
4 Fitzhardinge Street, London W1H 0AH

Contents

Introduction

'The recording of an experience in colour is deeply satisfying as conscious, unconscious meanings for visual, verbal, tactile and kinetic sensations become interrelated. This may produce a positive development, or a means of clearing conflict in the fabric of experience.'

Ruth Shaw

Finger painting has traditionally been thought of only as an activity for the very young, or as therapy for the mentally or physically handicapped. Both these uses are considered in this book, as they are obviously important, but they do not tell the whole story: like any other art form finger painting can be used in many different ways.

As a painting experience, finger paint is 'at the beginning' for it is a direct and natural medium, like clay. Both materials are manipulated by the hands with the need of few auxiliary tools, and both permit images to be quickly re-shaped as ideas change and crystallize. By their very nature they allow initial success, which is tremendously important when beginning any creative activity with children: from a successful start much can be achieved, but failure often turns a child against drawing or painting.

The changing development of the child from pre-school through to adolescence is the theme of this book, and it illustrates how the activity of finger painting can be adapted to these varying stages of growth. Of course finger painting is only one of many activities, and should be considered alongside other movement-related forms of art, such as drama and music.

◀ **2** Creative activities where the children can learn about their physical selves. The spontaneous use of particular hand shapes re-occur in all these activities

Historical notes

Before discussing finger painting in education it should be emphasized that a precedent is not being created when brushes are discarded and pictures created by using hands, fingers, pieces of cloth, and bits of card or stick. Artists have always used their hands as an extension of their painting tools, in order to achieve unusual effects.

Primitive man communicated by painting and drawing symbols on the walls of his cave, with his fingers, and printing hand shapes onto these designs (figure 3). His pots were also decorated with simple thumb prints, stick impressions and twisted cord.

Throughout recorded history, various forms of 'finger painting' have been used. At Pompeii imprints of a thumb mark left in the paint stucco, once part of a wall decoration, can still be seen. And Pliny, in his *Natural History*, describes the 'great ones' and the 'lesser ones'. The latter painted with brushes, but the 'great ones', using an encaustic technique, applied melted wax with a spatula to their battleships, houses, and to the gladiators' chariots.

◀ **3**   The symbolic use of the hands in primitive art: an aboriginal wall painting, with the artist's hands used as a stencil
Australian News and Information Bureau

11

Similarly in the East – in the eighth century AD the Chinese painter Ching Isao created pictures using his fingers to produce both figurative drawings and graphic symbols.

Leonardo da Vinci, famous for his experiments, tried many different methods of transferring paint onto canvas or paper, recording the results in his detailed work *Speculative Invention of Accidental Blots and Stains*.

Print makers, too, have always been noted for the unconventional ways in which they apply colour; and it is interesting to note how Rembrandt, William Blake, Whistler and later the French Impressionists enriched their drawings and illustrations by unorthodox techniques of applying paint.

Paul Klee is a more recent example of an artist using experimental methods: he worked directly onto glass, and also incorporated printed surfaces into many of his paintings (figure 4).

Artists today are constantly developing new ways of working and new methods of applying paint to canvas. Tachisme, as illustrated in the works of Jackson Pollock, has as its guiding philosophy the same basic considerations as finger painting – the enrichment of a surface through direct manipulation of the paint on that surface.

Finger painting in education

In the early 1920s, when education was ripe for experimentation and new activities, Ruth Shaw introduced finger painting to the children in her Rome school. She wanted to create a material that would enable the children to translate their thoughts directly onto paper. Using clay or starch as a base and experimenting with all sorts of materials, she searched for a form of paint that was non-toxic, harmless, soluble in water and, above all, like the natural play element, mud. With the development

4 *Child Consecrated to Suffering:* oil on canvas by Paul Klee. The 'textures'
were made by placing paper on wet paint and pulling it off again
Albright-Knox Art Gallery, Buffalo, New York

of this different type of paint, which was unlike the tradi-
tional oil or tempera colour, came the beginning of finger
painting as an educational activity (figures 6 and 7).

In the late 1930s Ruth Shaw exhibited her children's
paintings in America where they created great interest,
especially among educational psychologists. Her book
Finger Painting, written in 1938, outlines her early experiments, and it is still of interest today because it records
the specific reactions of children to finger painting.

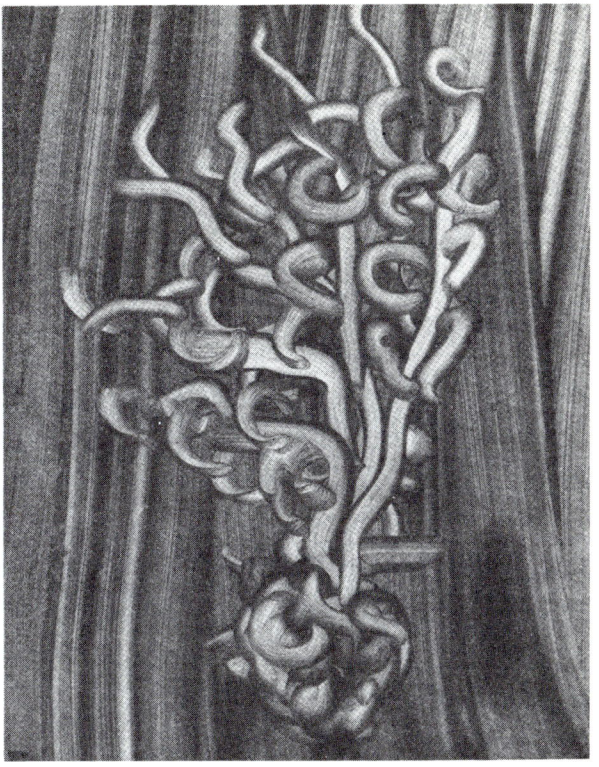

6 *Four Saints of the Church* (age twelve)
Examples of finger paintings done by children at Ruth
Shaw's school in Rome in 1933:

7 Abstract entitled *China* (age ten)
Little Brown and Company, Boston

In Great Britain and America finger painting is still, unfortunately, regarded mainly as an infant school activity, with few teachers realizing its great potential, particularly as an introduction to print making. In the following pages various finger painting activities are explored, both as infant school experiments, and as project activities for the middle and upper schools.

◀ **5** *Man and Dog:* ink monoprint with added collage by Jean Dubuffet. The man and dog were created by cutting out paper shapes and using them as stencils over the inked plate
Pierre Matisse Gallery, New York Rights reserved ADAGP Paris 1972

15

Pre-school

'There is little one can teach a child about finger painting but everything to learn.'

Ruth Shaw

Fingers were invented before brushes. This simple statement is the key to finger painting as a play activity for the very young child, who will stick his fingers into his food, make patterns in mud or sand, and draw on steamed-up windows. These intuitive reactions are the beginnings of a child's play experience.

Some of the most significant stages in a child's creative development take place in the pre-school years, and it is important to encourage him to draw and paint before he goes to school. Finger painting is an ideal method to start with – children of this age will naturally make marks with their fingers when using paint, and one can see examples of pictures done at this stage which include fingermarks, thumb prints and even hand prints as part of the design (figures 8–17).

8–10 A two-and-a-half-year-old's first exploration into the world of finger paint. Note the protective apron and formica kitchen table: in this situation he can explore the feel of the paint freely (see figures 27–36 for method of working)

11–13 At first his reactions are very tentative, with one finger and then one hand. Gradually as he gains more confidence the arc of his hand widens. The colours are explored separately, but soon they become intermixed and new colours appear, as if by magic. This can be a most positive introduction to colours and their names

14–16 Both hands are now being used and the child has become very involved in his play. Hand prints are made and he soon discovers how a single finger can also make interesting marks in the paint. The resulting circles are the beginnings of all children's drawings. With added confidence more complicated circles are created and destroyed

17 The child now looks for encouragement and praise to motivate new activity. Here simple pattern prints could be made to continue the play situation

Parents should try to understand the value of un-influenced drawing and painting at this age. What to them is just scribbling with fingers in the paint is, for the child, a natural part of developing. As he gains more control certain shapes reoccur, circles and ovals which in turn become everything from his mother to a house or a ship (figures 18–25). Finger paint provides the child with a material which will enable him to develop his drawings to the next stage, where colour predominates.

Another important consideration in encouraging pre-school finger painting is that, although the painting is usually finished in a short time, the child can easily wipe it out with his hand and start all over again. This destructive urge is just as meaningful as the creative one which first started the drawing (see figures 87–9).

Getting dirty is also very much a part of a child's development, and if it can occur in this type of situation he will gain a positive introduction to colour and texture as well. If a child goes to school with only limited tactile experience much creative work will be restricted through a dislike of handling certain materials.

Finger painting at home

The kitchen area makes an ideal environment for finger painting, as the kitchen table with formica top is a suitable working surface, and as the mother is usually working there too she can provide initial help. If simple prints are made these should be displayed if possible, as an additional encouragement (see figures 27–36 for outline of method of working, figures 40–5 for making a print).

18–25 A child of three-and-a-half already has more confidence to produce a wider range of marks. Both hands are freely used as well as parts of the hands, including the palms, finger tips and forearms. The circle patterns are also more complex and will soon become pictures and patterns that have definite titles and descriptions ▶

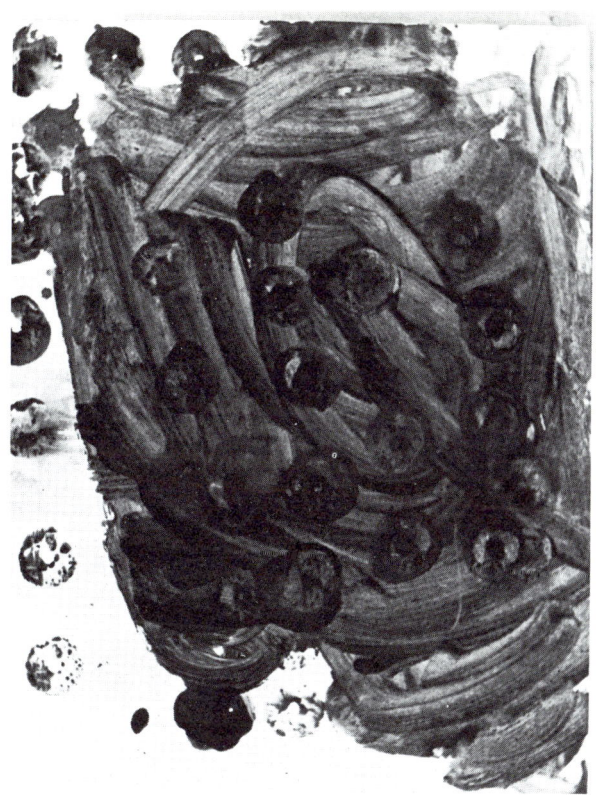

26a A very early finger painting using powder colour mixed with paste. Finger prints, thumb prints and direct painting using a cork have all been used to make a pattern

26b This portrait is a print taken from a first-phase finger painting in an infant class. It was crayoned to give added interest and to introduce other materials to the child's picture making

Nursery and infant school

In a well-organized infant school the child really comes into his own. Here he finds not only skilled teachers but also a classroom full of bricks, sand, water, wax crayons, paint, clothes to dress up in, houses and shops to play in, and musical instruments on which to explore sounds and rhythm.

Finger paint takes its place as part of this environment, as it allows the child to explore the feel of paint directly with very few rules or restrictions. Giving a child tools often hampers freedom of expression – for example, a pencil is gripped too firmly to allow the free flow of ideas – so in this context finger paint has few rivals.

Preparation
Young children have no concept of messiness, so it is important to create an area in the classroom which is easily cleaned and is also near a sink.

Finger painting is not a viable activity for forty children at a time. A good idea is to set up a special area in a corner of the room (obviously this is more easily accomplished in an open-plan school than in a formal classroom). However, as prints can be developed and cut out for friezes etc this does extend the activity so that all the children can take turns to finger paint (figures 37, 38, 39).

Working surfaces: in the initial stages the work should be large and uninhibited, and this requires a table with a smooth top, such as formica. A plastic cover, a piece of linoleum or gloss-painted hardboard are also suitable surfaces on which to work. It is important that the table is high enough to enable the child to work standing up, as this position provides greater freedom of movement.

Clothing: a protective overall or smock should be worn with the sleeves rolled up.

Paint and materials: in the nursery-school stage finger paste can be pre-mixed by the teacher using powder colour as the pigment, and starch or glue as the binder. This recipe is satisfactory for initial experiments, simple combed designs, etc but it does tend to stain and is not so easily handled as the specially formulated paint, which is relatively inexpensive.

Finger paint is manufactured commercially and can be bought through the normal educational suppliers, as well as from retail shops (see list of main suppliers on page 95). It is smooth in consistency, comes in a variety of colours, and has the additional advantages of being highly soluble, easily rinsed from the hands and non-toxic.

The only other materials needed are a spatula or spoon, a bowl of water, and a sponge or cloth to clean down the surface when work is completed.

Outline of working: if the children have not done any finger painting before, demonstrate the amount of paint required and the method of dispensing it onto the surface (for they tend to use more paint than is necessary). Two colours are adequate and in these early experiments the children should be allowed to work spontaneously.

The hands and table top should be cleaned between pictures and the tops replaced on the jars of paint when not in use.

27 The correct 'set up' for finger painting: the formica surface is wet, ready to begin

28 For these first experiments two colours are sufficient

29 The colours are now intermixed. A small amount of paint covers a large area when smoothed out; note both hands are being used

30 Even hand prints will produce interesting effects

31 The finger tips will also make complicated patterns

32 The whole body is now being used to make sweeping marks

33 The fingers used in a different way to make scaley patterns

34 The pattern is destroyed ready to start again

35 The sides of the hands make more sophisticated lines

36 From these marks and lines paintings appear, sometimes
by accident and sometimes deliberately

37 Nursery school frieze: 90 cm × 60 cm (3 ft × 2 ft). The trees were cut out of simple combed patterns, with the figures and birds added afterwards

38 Detail of a flower frieze, 60 cm × 240 cm (2 ft × 8 ft), using a large finger paint print for the background. The flowers were crayoned

39 *The Easter Egg Tree:* 90 cm × 240 cm (3 ft × 8 ft). To make the tree all the children in the class printed off a simple finger paint pattern. These were then cut out and crayoned to make the eggs. The trunk was printed directly onto the frieze paper

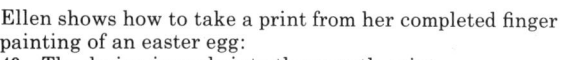

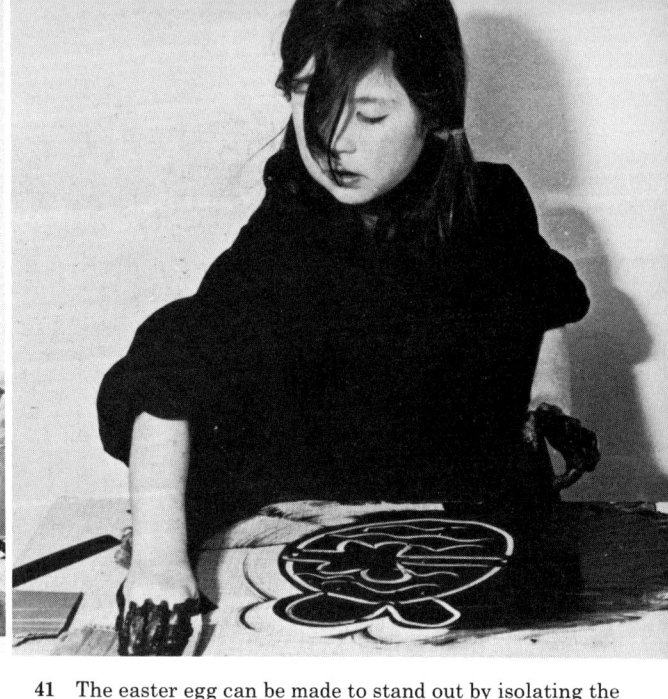

Ellen shows how to take a print from her completed finger painting of an easter egg:

40 The design is made into the smooth paint

42 The finished finger painting. Ellen cleans her hands ready to print

41 The easter egg can be made to stand out by isolating the shape, using a piece of card or wood to scrape away the unwanted paint

43 Thin detail paper or lining paper is then laid over the design and smoothed down with the palm of the hand

Plate 1 Large decorative collage bird – 135 cm × 90 cm (4 ft 6 in. × 3 ft). This was created by a group of student teachers, using many different types of textured prints to produce the feathered body and wings. In this method of work very early finger painting experiments can be incorporated

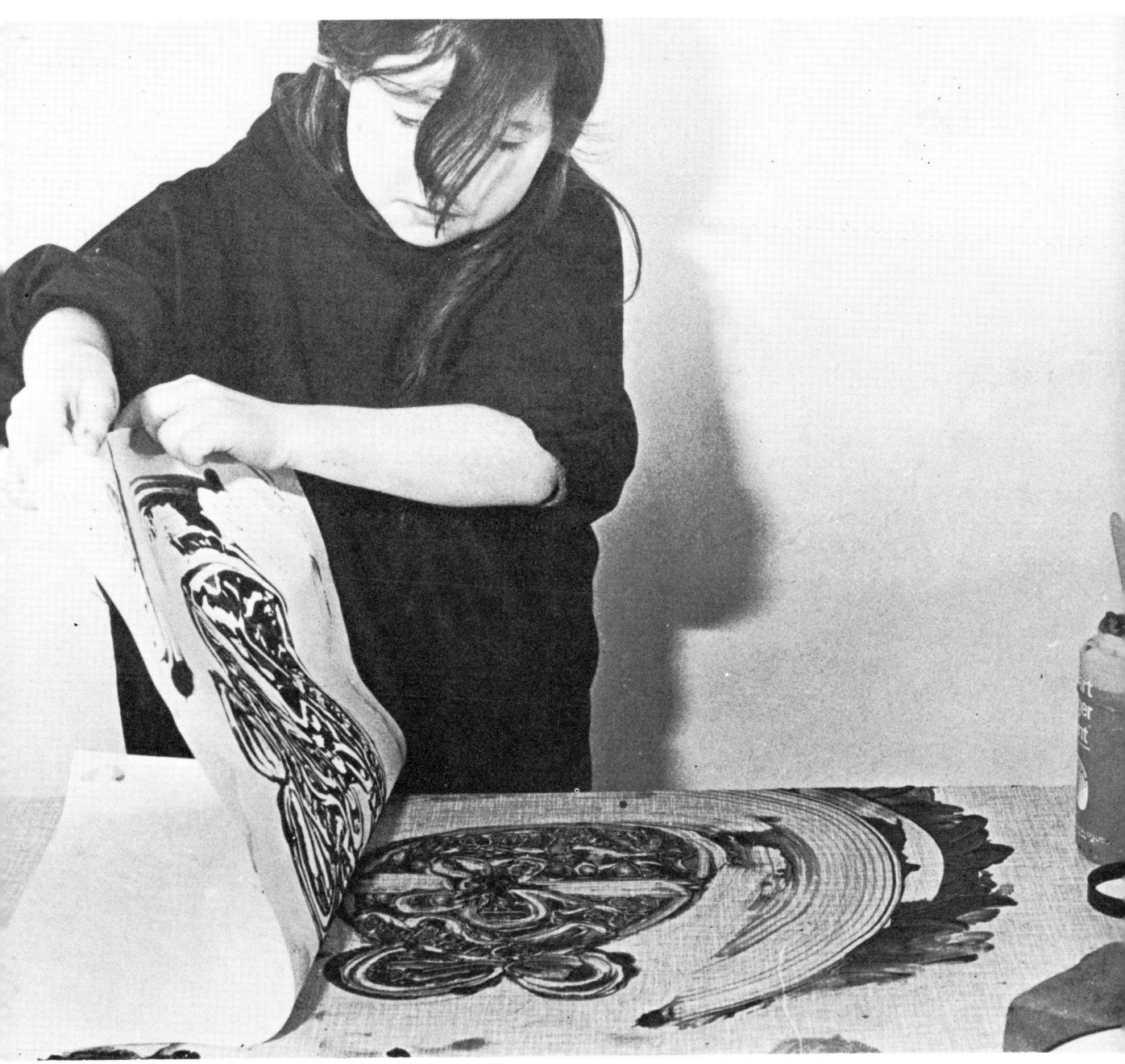

44 The finished print is then pulled off slowly. If the first print is not smoothed down too heavily, at least two prints can be taken

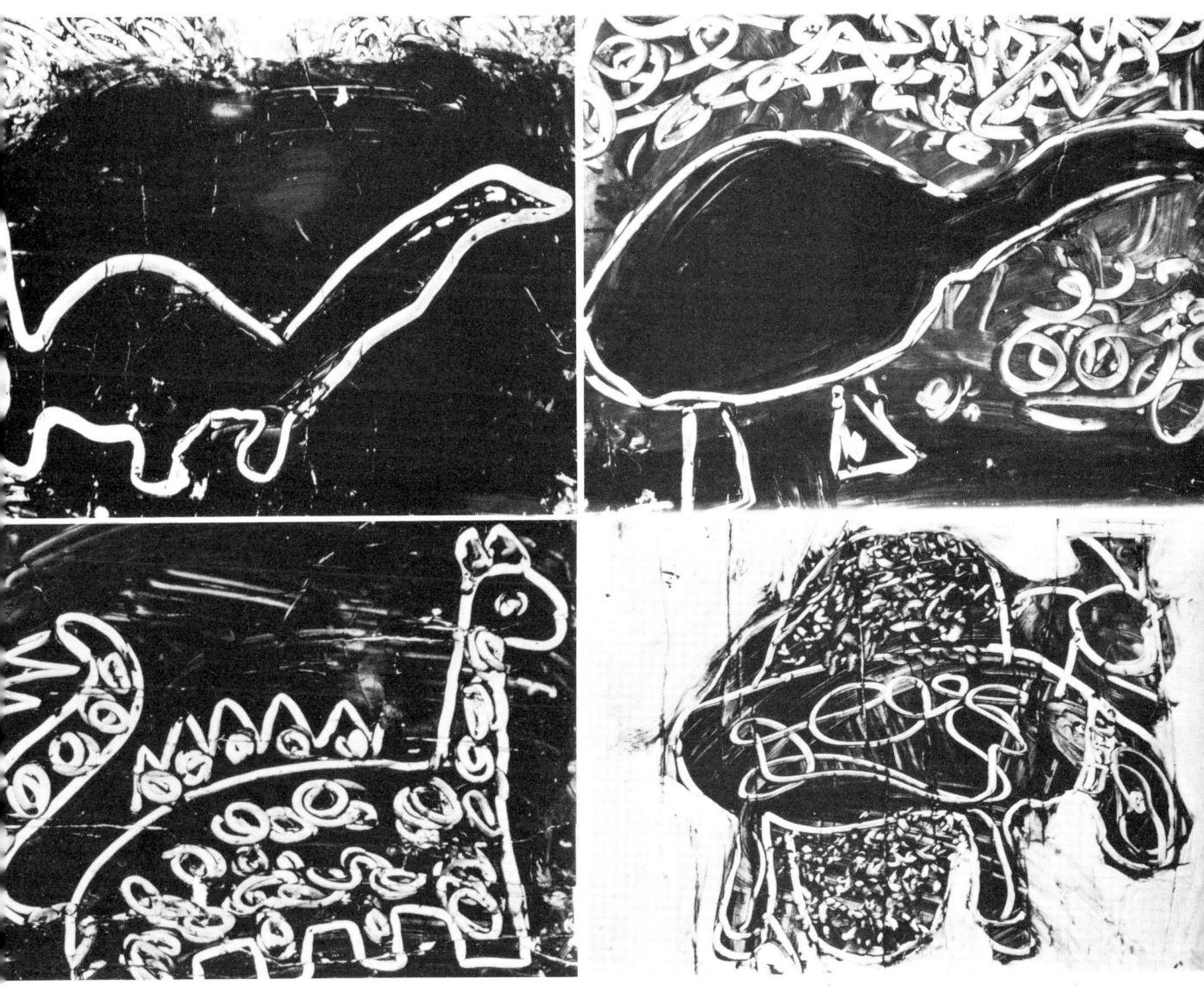

46–9 Prehistoric monsters: note how the pictures become more complicated as the children become more confident

◀ **45** The surface is now cleaned down ready for the next child to paint

Activities related to finger painting

Finger painting should never be considered as an isolated activity. In a lively school the children are encouraged to talk about their paintings, and to write about them – a tape-recorder can be the ideal means of recording these impressions.

The teacher can also change the emphasis of 'story time' by actually illustrating the main characters in the story with finger paint. This is an excellent way of obtaining the children's undivided attention (figure 50).

Radio and television programmes, or a visit to a museum, will create a wealth of ideas for subjects which can quickly be translated into finger paintings (figures 51–8). This way of painting encourages immediate participation, and even the most hesitant child will find that his pattern can be used as part of a larger group frieze, or as a cover for a class book. At the other extreme the highly gifted child might find some difficulty in adapting to the new material, but he will soon build up a vocabulary of textures and marks, and may possibly develop his ideas much further than he would have if given only familiar materials with which to work.

At this stage it can be seen how creative writing, mime, drama, movement and dance resemble this way of painting, as they are all spontaneous and personal to the individual child. This being so, it is most important that the freedom of the activity is emphasized, not the end products. In the infant school children should be given a variety of materials with which they can express themselves in different ways. What happens to the child as a result of these experiences is what matters, not the actual work produced.

Finger painting should not be thought of as just messing around before 'real' painting begins. Giving every child the chance of being involved will often give him enough

50 Simple illustration of a dragon made by the teacher to illustrate the story *The Desperate Dragon*. This picture is then wiped out ready for the next part of the story

self-confidence to start other skills such as reading and writing. Indeed, the body rhythms emphasized by the painting are ideal pre-writing exercises, and can be used to produce many different left to right writing patterns

51 Moon collage using a group finger painting as a beginning

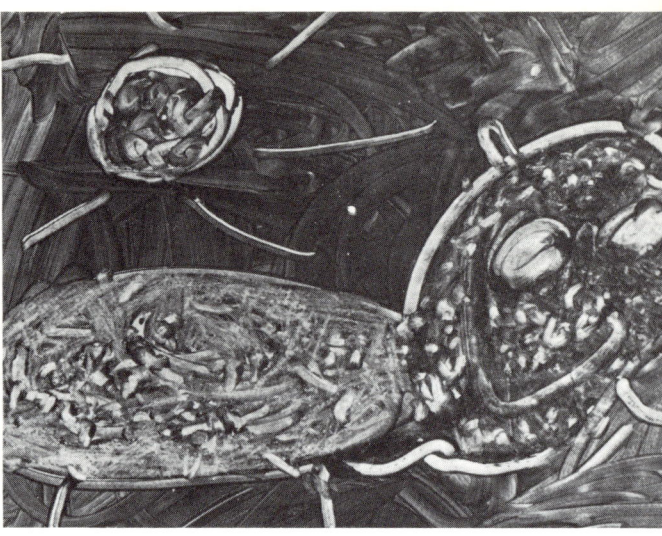

52 *Gobbolino* the Witches' Cat, an illustration from *Story Time*

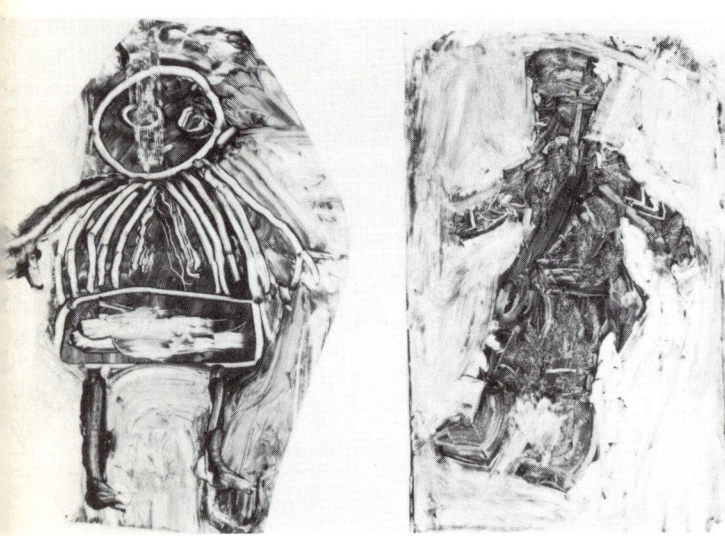

53 'People I would like to be': a dancer and a soldier

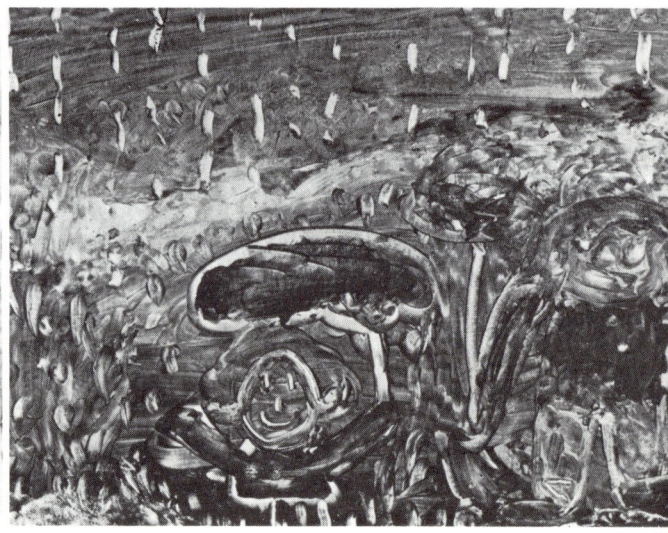

54–6 Finger paintings using 'rain' as the motivation. A rain machine was made and rain noises recorded. To complete the project words were made up to describe rain, and finger paintings used to illustrate all the words and feelings about the rain

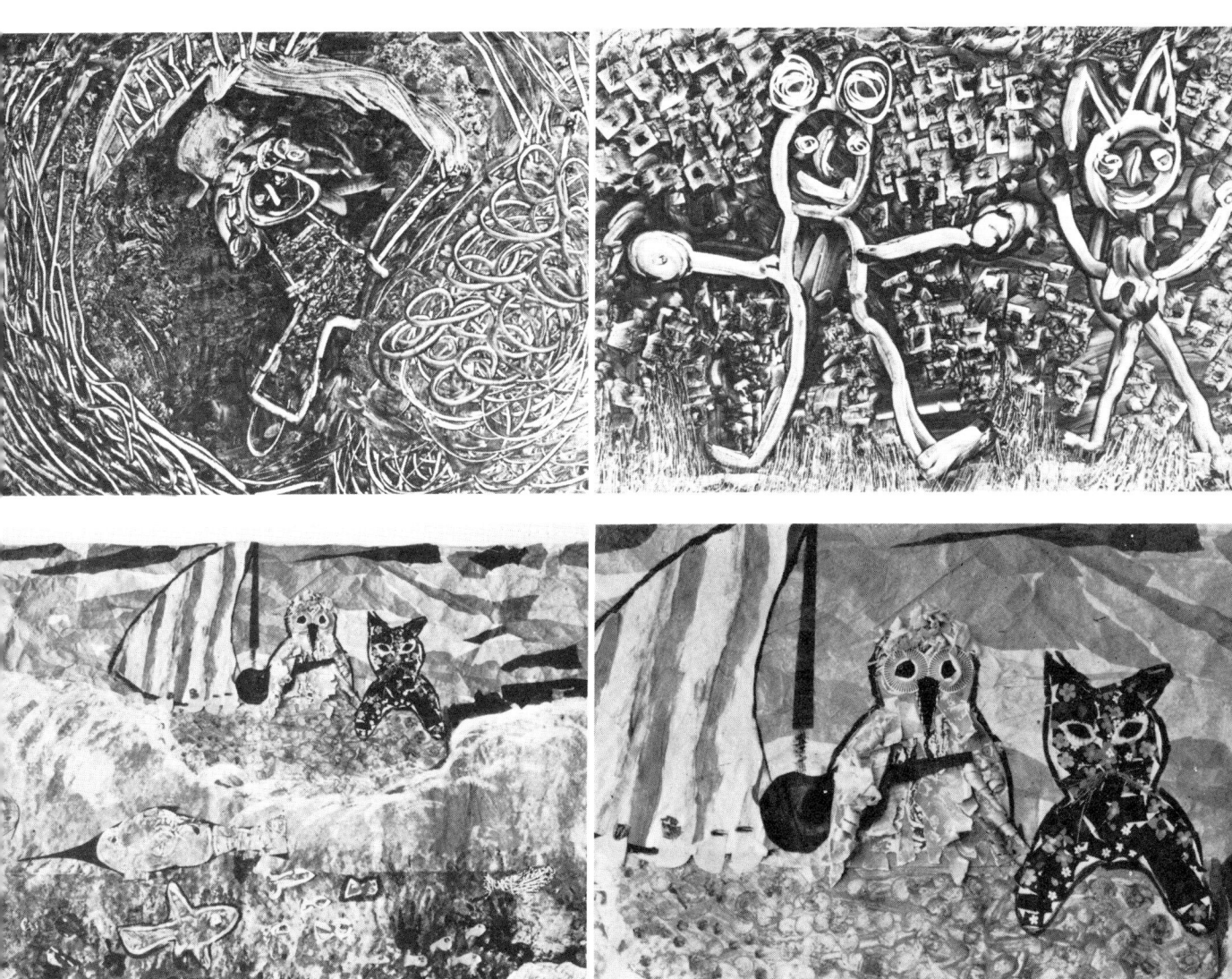

57–8 A large decorative mural (and a detail from it) on the theme of *The Owl and the Pussy Cat*. Decorative prints taken from finger paintings were used for most of the design, with collage materials and powder colour added to emphasize the main figures. To establish the scale of the mural, small hand prints appear all over the bottom of the sea

39

The transition
to the primary stage

In the pre-school and infant stages finger painting is used as part of the play situation, to help the child acquire a wide range of experiences: the activity is purely experimental with little structure or development. In fact, all finger painting should start with a period of experimentation (figure 59), as this not only allows the young artist to get into a creative mood after other activities, but also encourages him to express his ideas freely before committing himself.

The painting activities discussed and illustrated so far have been completed directly onto a smooth topped table, with the child either rubbing out his design so that he can create a new one, or taking a simple monoprint, as shown in figures 40–5. (The process of monoprinting is a very good one for this age group, as there is no limitation on size, and the technique allows big backgrounds and images to be created quickly, speed being a most important consideration in the primary school.) But as the child grows older he will naturally want to develop his work further.

59 All finger painting should start with a period of experimentation

60 *Lizard:* finger painting print on cellophane by a six-year-old girl. Finger paint was mixed with acrylic

The introduction of finger paint paper is a useful development at this stage, for it allows the original painting to be retained. This technique is illustrated and described in figures 61–5. Finger paint paper is manufactured commercially and is a 'coated' paper which allows the finger paint to move smoothly over the surface. When dry the paint is absorbed slightly into the surface and is thus retained.

Experiments with different types of surfaces, such as plastic and washable wallpapers, can also produce interesting results. If the paint flakes off, add a little acrylic medium to the colour.

Another interesting extension of finger painting for this age group would be the introduction of a variety of simple collage techniques and paper constructions, which allow the child to experiment with texture and colour, and produce more exciting assembled pictures and sculptural forms (see figures 51, 57, 66).

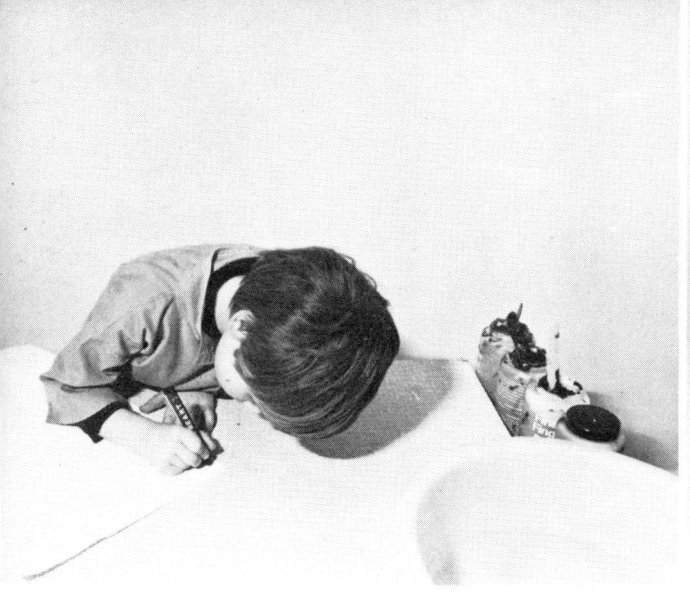

Daniel uses finger paint paper so that he can retain the original painting instead of taking a print. The process of working is exactly the same as finger painting directly onto the table: the only extras are a bowl of cold water, or a sink near at hand, and some finger paint paper:

61 Mark the shiny side of the finger paint paper so that it can be recognized when both sides are wet

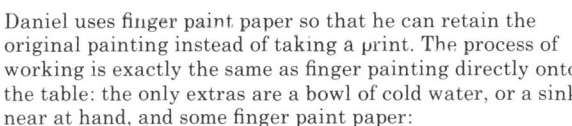

62 Completely immerse the paper under the water

64 Spread the paint all over the paper with the base of the hand allowing the paint to go over the edges. This is most important if a free flow of movement is to be obtained. Experiment with the fingers, hands and forearms. Variations of pressure will give tonal contrasts in the paint giving an illusion of depth. If the painting becomes too dry sprinkle the surface of the paint with water

63 Smooth down the paper carefully (shiny side uppermost) so that there are no wrinkles, or air bubbles. Moisten the surface of the paper again if it is too dry

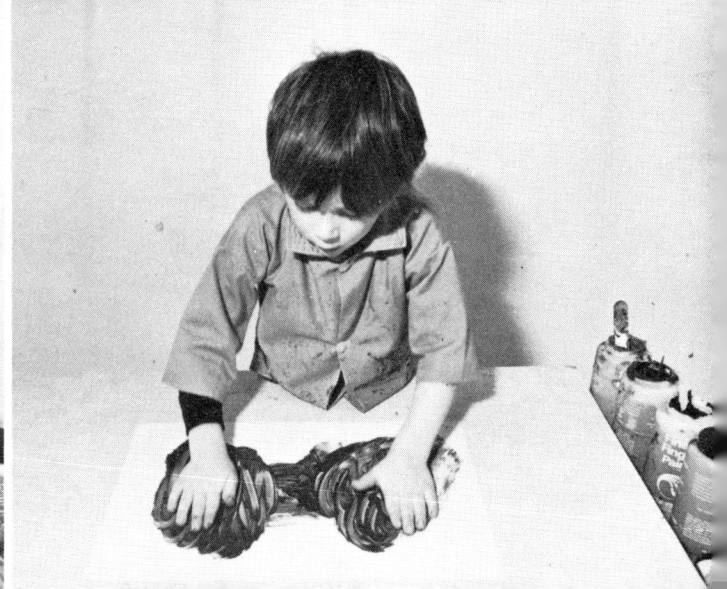

65 When the painting is completed lift by two corners and lay on newspaper to dry. If it wrinkles place the painting face down onto newspaper and apply a warm iron

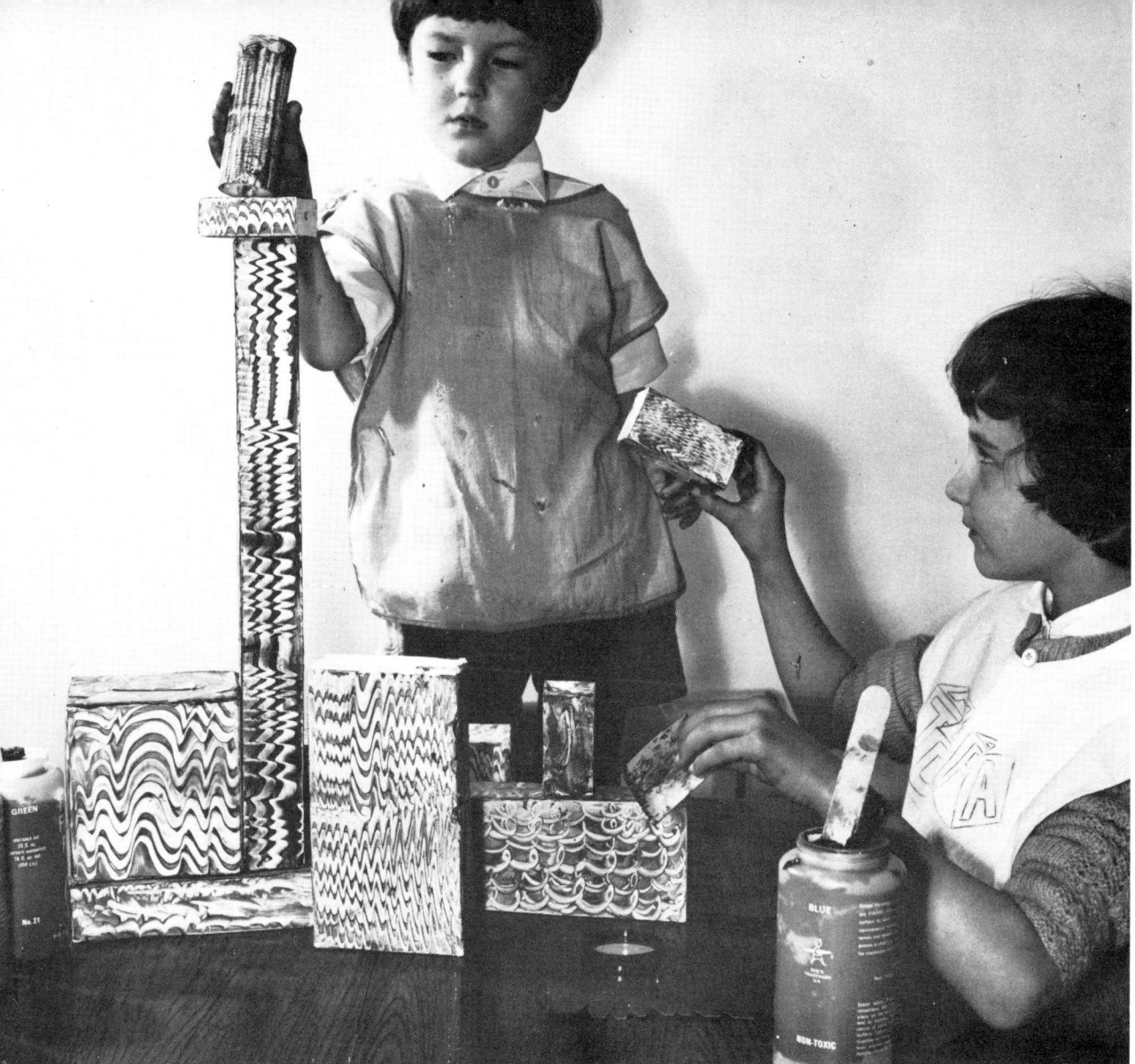

66 Three-dimensional finger paintings have been made into various shaped boxes. First the boxes were painted with white emulsion paint. When dry the finger paint designs were made directly onto the various surfaces, each face being a different colour. Sometimes the fingers were used to make the patterns, and sometimes a simple cardboard comb.

When dry these decorative forms were varnished with a diluted acrylic medium so that they could be easily handled.

A variety of constructions can be made using these shapes, as well as the bodies for assembled cardboard sculptures (see figures 76–9). Decorative gift boxes can also be made in this way

Finger painting with seven to eleven year olds

Texture

As we have seen children will naturally start finger paintings in line, using only one finger. The teacher should now try and encourage them to experiment, and to start using a variety of marks and textures in their drawings. In this work it is important to outline the basic method of working, but it is equally important not to emphasize a particular set of techniques. Once the paint has been smoothed out get the children to see how many different patterns they can make using their finger tips, sides of hands, palms, knuckles, nails, and even the forearm to produce large sweeping marks. The spatula used to spoon out the paint and the old rags used to clean down the tables will also make a new range of textures, as will corrugated cardboard, pieces of hessian, string and bits of polystyrene (figures 67, 68, 70, 71). In turn these experiments into 'textures' can be carried on when using other art materials such as wax crayons, powder colour, inks, clay, etc.

As the children explore these endless ways of making textures encourage them to record them logically by taking prints: the most inexpensive paper can be used. Keep all the prints, no matter how simple, as they can always be used later for collages and friezes. As can be

67 Ships. An experiment into texture which has been carried on when using wax crayons and powder colour mixed with detergent. To achieve the effect of the rough sea, the pattern has been scratched through the paint, using the wrong end of a paint brush

Plate 2   *Demetrius* – 60 cm × 45 cm (2 ft × 1 ft 6 in.) by Jane
Gabrielle Scott. In this three-dimensional paper sculpture
dragon the artist has used many different types of finger
paint and printed textures. To achieve the effect of scales
the various papers were first curled before being assembled
over a rolled newspaper frame

seen (figures 69, 72–5) these sheets of textural experiments can be used in a variety of ways – sometimes cut up, sometimes torn, and sometimes overprinted with found shapes to create new and interesting surfaces.

Full participation in the activity is the most important aspect of this type of work. Drawing a picture and then colouring it allows little development, for a young child will usually not have the confidence to alter and improve it. But the method of assembling pictures out of textures enables a process of constant reassessment, so that the work is not finished until the child is satisfied with it.

Colour

For these initial experiments there is no need to talk about colour or colour mixing. The children should be allowed to choose which colour they like best, and if two colours are used they will soon discover simple colour mixing for themselves. Colour work should always start in this subjective way, and then through experiment can come discussion about which range of colours is most suitable for a particular painting (ie cold colours: blues, greens, blacks and violet; hot colours: red, yellow, orange and certain greens).

With the introduction of large projects and friezes the children can be encouraged to work in groups, sharing their prints and assembling a joint effort (figures 77–9). This is an important step, and an easy way of teaching them how to work together. Finger painting should always be a beginning for art (and other) activities, never a closed technique (figure 80).

◀ 68 This print records a design which has been made using not only all the fingers but also the palm and sides of the hand

69 A decorative bird, assembled from a wide variety of finger paint textures. Rubbings and overprinted shapes have also been added to enrich the completed design

Another method of making interesting prints:
71 First experiments using an old scrubbing brush to make textures into the paint (any object can be used)

70 Using corrugated card onto finger paint paper produces a strong linear design

72 Torn paper shapes are laid onto the paint surface to make the design

73 The design is then built up as large as the paper used for printing, and more paper is added to isolate the design

75 The paper is removed carefully to reveal the design. The torn paper has acted as a mask to create areas of white in contrast with the highly textural printed surfaces

74 The print is taken in the usual way

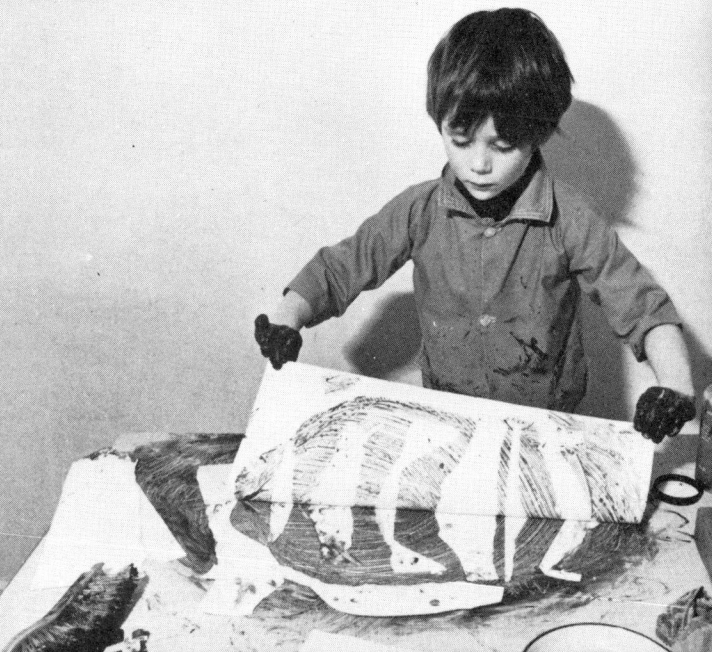

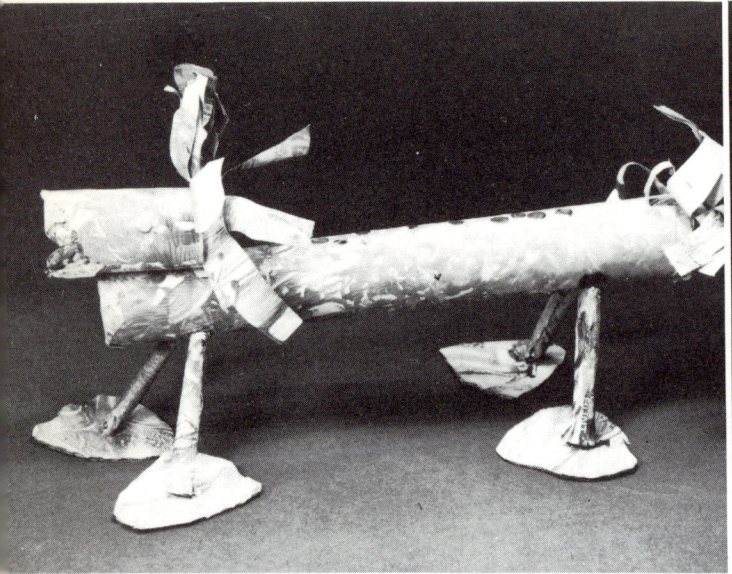

76 Animal form from finger paint textures glued onto cardboard cylinders

77 Simple paper sculpture figures based on cones. These can be used as puppets or as three-dimensional forms, in front of a group mural

78 Using decorative printed boxes and papers the train and driver were made as part of a group project on 'Travel'

79 A three-dimensional head of a mythical warrior, the framework being made from chicken wire. These particular finger paint textures were specifically printed for this project, whereas in figures 76–8 free patterns were used as appropriate

Pictorial work

Parallel to this exploration of colour and texture comes the child's eagerness to give form to his own figurative ideas. Pencil and ordinary paint tend to be rather limiting, as with them the child will probably only be able to repeat familiar images and subject matter, because he is uncertain how to progress. The particular attraction of finger paint is that the child is in physical contact with the actual paint surface, and therefore in complete control to embellish or destroy the patterns and images he creates. To be able to wipe out an evil monster and create a familiar train or clown gives him confidence over himself, and enables continual experiment until he produces a painting he wants to keep (figures 87–9). Finger painting allows the logical development of a new range of images, and the child will very quickly be introducing curls and beards to his portraits, or drawing slimy scales on prehistoric monsters (figures 90–4).

80 Finger painting as a play activity at home. A commentary from the artist as he or she works gives added amusement, as it allows new characters and detail to be described as they are included, in the same way as captions are used in a strip cartoon. When completed the pictures are either printed or wiped out ready for the next animated story

81–2 The development of very spontaneous figurative finger painting. The full use of the body has allowed the linear rhythm of the picture to flow from one side of the picture

surface to the other. Although only small areas of texture have been added the painting is well composed and full of interest

83 The outline of the Viking was first printed onto detail paper, which was then cut and mounted onto newspaper to strengthen it. The design was then worked into using paint and collage, the completed figure being used as part of a frieze

84 A Chinese mask printed onto thin cardboard. Contrasting textures were added to give the design a three-dimensional quality

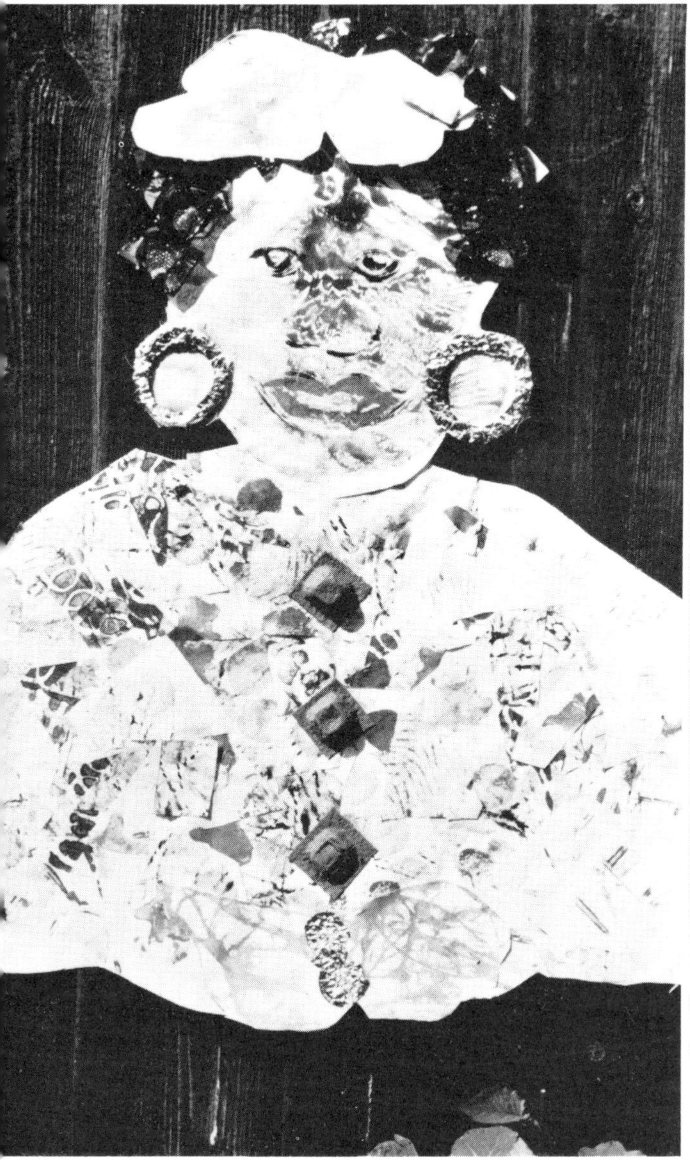

85 A simple collage figure using printed textures as a paper mosaic

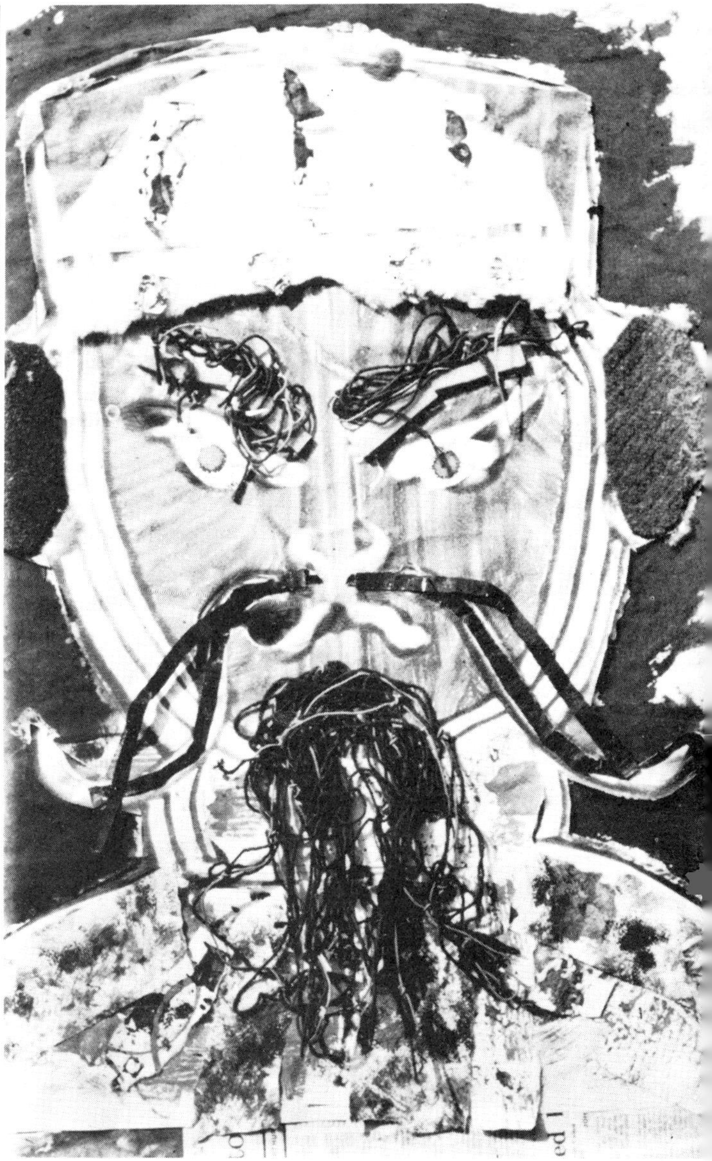

86 A Chinese warrior, using a finger paint print as the background. Interesting collage materials such as string, cloth and tin foil were then added to give the design more life

87–9 A very important development stage in a child's picture making: Ellen has produced something which does not completely satisfy her but, unlike conventional painting, her picture can be quickly eradicated and a new one started. This freedom of expression is one of the most important reasons for using finger paint, as it allows new images to grow and develop without fear of making mistakes

90–4 The development of a painting, from simple basic circular forms to the finished printed picture; it is interesting to see how the early drawing is built up entirely of circles. Gradually as the painting progresses and new tools are introduced, in this case a piece of cardboard, the animal changes and becomes more exciting and lively.

Note how the young artist washes his hands before taking the first print. If he prints carefully two or three images can be taken, as well as a positive print from the first printed sheet. This way of working is made possible because the first print will pick up too much finger paint, which can easily be printed off onto another piece of paper

Gradually the child's images change and become more like those of an adult – he will become more aware of his surroundings, and more conscious of trying to make things 'look right'. Instead of teaching adult concepts like perspective, however, it is much better to introduce new materials and new ways of working. Finger painting encourages a wider approach, in creating pictures which have both texture and a variety of colours (figures 95–101) and, as we have seen, the prints taken can be developed in a number of ways (figures 103–6).

Print making, and finger painting generally, are useful methods of extending the particular subject matter and behaviour patterns of the primary stage into the more objective world of the middle school.

The two children work together to produce a large multi-coloured picture:

95–7 In this jungle scene a limited range of lighter colours are used for the background print – blue, yellow and green to create the sky, trees and grass. This free design using many different textural effects is then printed and put on one side

98–100 The table is cleaned down and dark colours such as black, red and violet smoothed out ready for the second print. More trees, as well as the main elephant and giraffe are then created in solid areas of colour so that they will show up over the lighter background print. The background print is then carefully placed over the animals and printed for the second time

101 The resulting print is always interesting as the under colours break through the textural areas of the second print to produce a completely new range of effects and colour tones. This method of producing multi-coloured prints can be developed by older pupils as the resulting prints resemble more sophisticated print processes such as lithography. If single areas of colour are used for each stage of the design pictures similar to progressive linocuts will be produced

102 The second and third prints from a finger painting often lack strength of detail, but can be enriched using crayons, inks and powder colour. In turn they can be cut out and mounted onto contrasting coloured papers, giving children the opportunity to develop one theme in many different ways

Middle school activities

With the gradual abolition of entrance examinations, and the introduction of middle and high schools, the transition between primary and secondary education is becoming less severe – but in most cases there is still a break, especially with art, which changes from a project activity to a timetable subject such as mathematics or English. In this context printing can be a tremendous help both for the art teacher, who has the problem of classes coming to him for only a very limited time each week, and for the pupils, as it can help them to succeed and thus gain confidence in their new surroundings.

It is most important that children of this age are given projects which allow them to do just this. They are often striving to make work look more realistic, and can consequently quickly become discouraged and lose confidence. Finger paint is a useful material for them because, by its very nature, it is not at all concerned with graphic realism – often an accident produces the most interesting effects so that the non-artist can achieve results as exciting as those of the more gifted student. As mistakes can be rectified in seconds it also allows continual experimentation to take place.

Printing never fails to stimulate children, and the methods described earlier (pages 54–57) can be used to

Opposite
Plate 3 An experimental design completed onto finger paint paper: part of a project on flowers by children of the Belthorn Primary School, Oswaldtwistle. At this stage finger paint paper can be used to achieve a completely new vocabulary of marks, utilizing all the different parts of the hand and forearm. This method lends itself to organic themes

create exciting and lively beginnings to paintings and murals (figures 108–10).

Assembled prints and collages also continue to be valuable activities for this age group as they extend the learning situation, allowing the students to build up their work gradually from very simple beginnings (figures 113–15).

In mid-adolescence many pupils will become dissatisfied with their lack of technique, especially using the more conventional forms of drawing. The technical side of finger painting can now be emphasized, not as a set of tricks, but as the tools for this particular art form.

With the re-introduction of finger paint paper, for instance, a whole new world of graphic experience may be explored, for the positive image can be kept as well as the negative. And monoprints can introduce a wide range of activities, from making simple line drawings to very sophisticated colour prints. Listed on page 66 are some monoprint projects, using finger paint.

It is also useful, at this stage, to take advantage of more experimental approaches to finger painting (see figures 118, 119). For example, inks can be added to a wet print to produce many exciting 'accidental' effects. Likewise finger paint, mixed with a little powder colour or liquid tempera, can be the basis of simple screen printing, using paper shapes as a mask.

If a polymer medium is mixed with the finger paint as a binder, paintings can be done on acetate sheets, plastic and glass. This sort of paint is much more durable than the ordinary finger paint, and can therefore be printed onto paper or thin card to be used for mobiles, Christmas decorations and other large-scale projects.

Monoprinting techniques suitable for use with finger paint

Number of colours	Method	Extensions
One or two colours	Produce design in line through the paint, using fingers, pieces of wood, etc.	Resulting print similar to a single colour linocut. Use different coloured papers, tissue, etc.
One or two colours	Produce design in a variety of textures, through the paint surface using marking tools.	Cut up or tear textures and use as beginnings of landscapes. Add paint and collage materials.
One colour black	Produce design in strong lines, using fingers or spatula.	Print off and develop using bright transparent inks or dyes. Print off using tissue papers to produce stained glass effect.
Dark colours	Smooth out paint thinly, cover with paper, draw image onto back of paper with stylus.	Print off, design appearing as line drawing on reverse side. Develop with paint.
Any number of colours	Experiment with paper shapes layed down onto paint surface which has been textured.	Print off, paper shapes will appear as white areas. Try moving paper shapes and print again. Use other types of masking shapes, ie string, hessian.
Any number of colours If paint is thick	Create design in strong relief. Print off.	Take a print of the first paper print. This will produce the positive image again. Print off as many designs as you can. Work into the fainter designs.
Different areas for different colours	Set up design like progressive linocut. Choose theme that does not require a close register, ie fishes in front of underwater scene or animals in a jungle. Work from light to dark.	Create background in lighter colours either realistic, ie jungle, water, rocks, sky, etc or as abstract texture. Print off. In dark paint create main front images. Isolate these images and then print onto background.

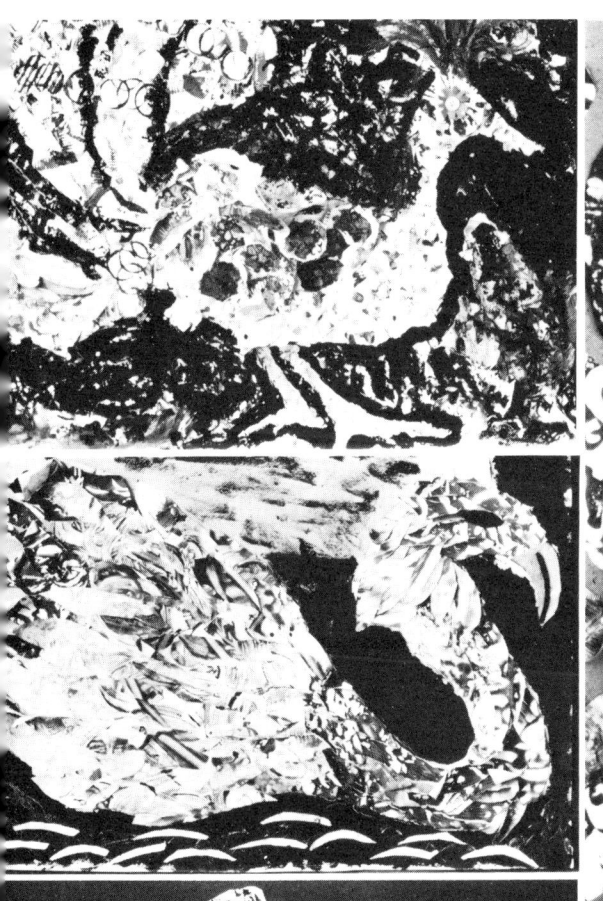

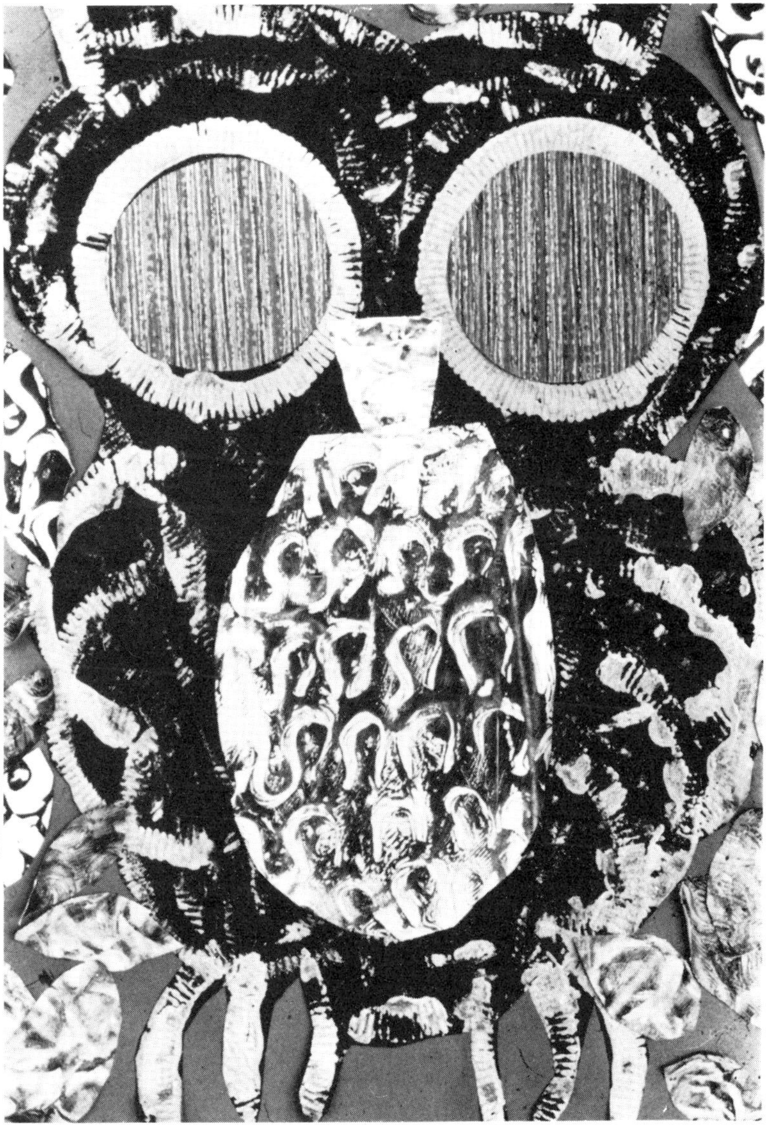

103-6 Different ways of developing the theme of birds, using second-phase prints as the starting point for the work. Thick paint, textured prints, corrugated card and various coloured papers were all used to enrich and develop the designs

107 Finger painting as a secondary school activity

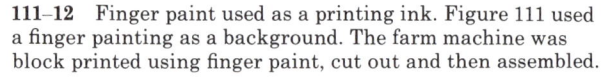

108–10 A more sophisticated print and resulting collage on the theme of a hedgehog. The enlargement shows the method of working

111–12 Finger paint used as a printing ink. Figure 111 used a finger painting as a background. The farm machine was block printed using finger paint, cut out and then assembled.

Figure 112 used finger paint as a printing ink. The various printing blocks were made out of corrugated card, hessian and a flat piece of cork

113–15 A series of fish paintings executed onto finger paint paper. This particular method of working was adopted as the designs were to be translated in a sgraffito technique onto ceramic tiles

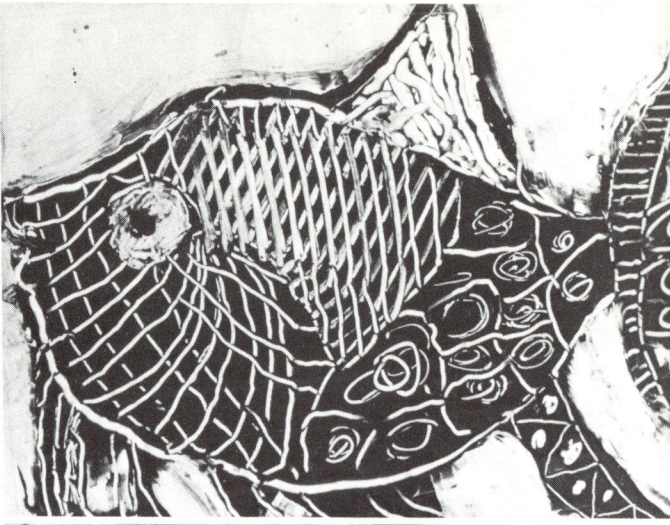

116–17 Experimental designs using the multi-printed technique. Many of these prints are complete in their own right. However some students might find them more interesting as beginnings for either figurative work or abstract paintings ▶

118–19 An interesting development from the basic
monoprinting technique, using finger paint, by Mary Mahan.
To achieve these designs a thin layer of dark finger paint
was first applied to the formica or glass. Over this was laid a
sheet of newsprint or detail paint. Using a pencil eraser the
image was then drawn onto the paper, resulting in a most
interesting line being transferred onto the reverse side of
the paper

120–1 Two prints from the same finger painting showing the variation of tone from the first print to the second print. Both pictures were used as the background for a project on Halloween

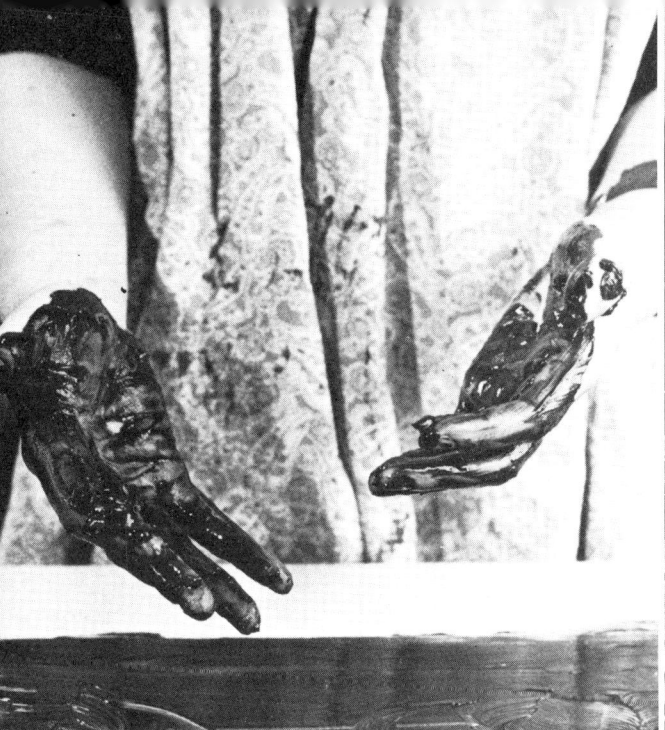

123–4 In mid-adolescence children need the opportunity to re-assess conventional art materials. Here finger paint is used to establish that paint has a definite textural surface instead of being just a flat colouring agent

The prints need not be used only as beginnings for a composition, but can be worked into with paint and inks to produce the final painting. Acrylic paints used in conjunction with collage will give the pupil another possible technique with which to maintain the initial freshness of the finger painting in the final work (figures 132–4).

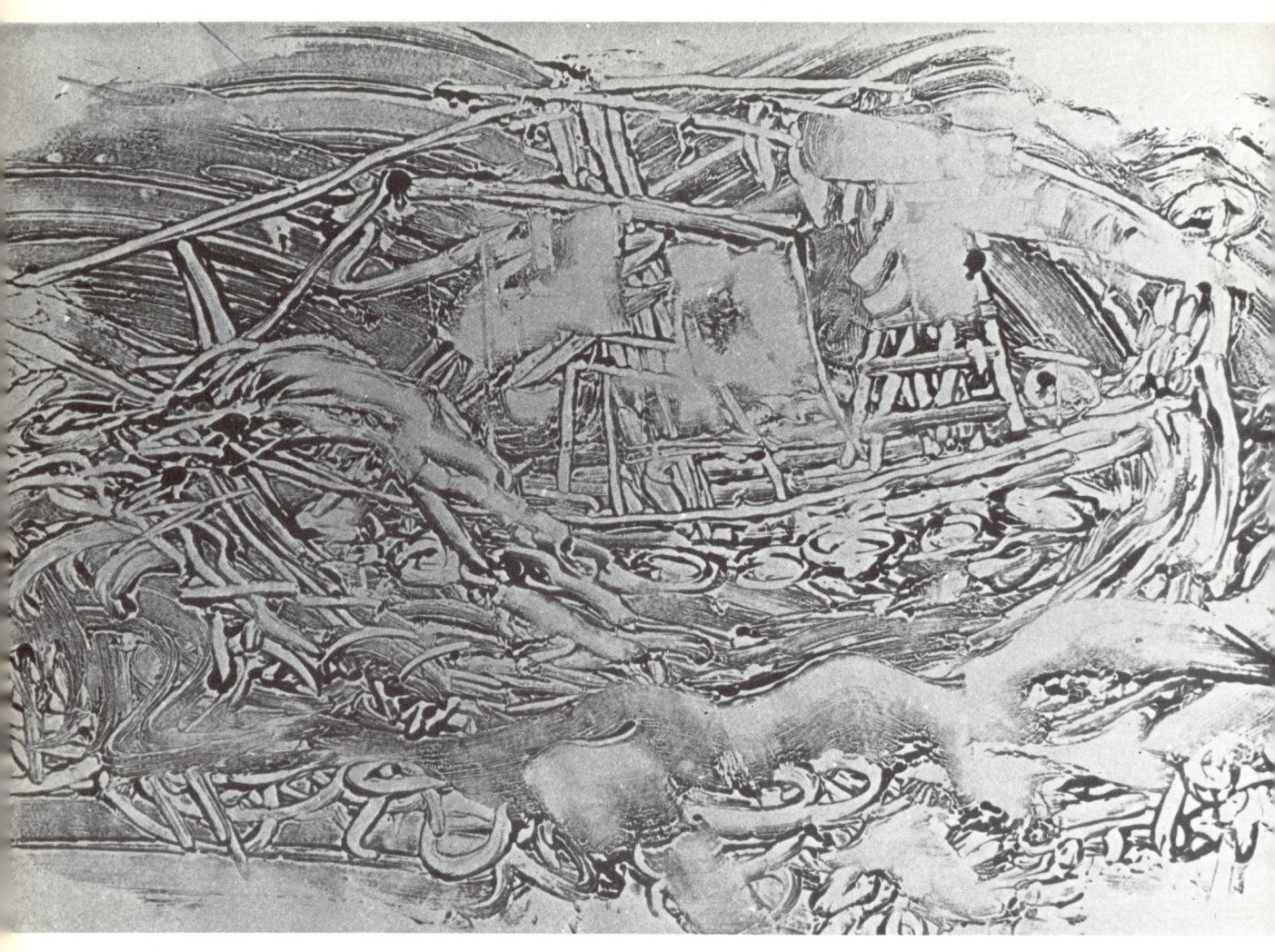

125 A large print, ready for development. The ship could be painted in a very realistic manner, using contrasting thicknesses of acrylic paint

Plate 4 Part of a 240 cm × 120 cm (8 ft × 4 ft) collage picture on the theme of the circus by a group of teachers at Twickenham Teachers' Centre. Multiple finger paintings were used for the basic drawings. Three prints of these weight-lifters were taken off the one design

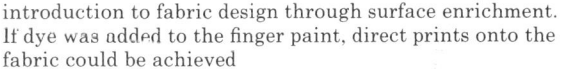

126–7 An exercise in linear rhythms: the student was asked to create a series of contrasting rhythms within the confines of the picture plane. This type of work is an excellent introduction to fabric design through surface enrichment. If dye was added to the finger paint, direct prints onto the fabric could be achieved

128–9 An extension of the work into linear rhythms: a variety of simple cardboard combs used as drawing tools. Basic letter forms, as an introduction to calligraphy, can also be introduced in this way

130–1 Using only black finger paint the basic concepts of optical art are explored. Prints taken from these experiments can be cut up and re-assembled to produce a completely new range of optical effects

132–4 Finger paint techniques used to produce a still life painting. Although the completed work is not photographically accurate, the student has been able to maintain the initial freshness of the drawing and has also been able to interpret the subject in a very personal way. Prints onto various coloured papers would give the artist a number of different images, which could then be developed. An extension of this way of working is to print a number of sheets in different colours which can then be cut up and re-assembled to produce the finished painting. This way of working is particularly interesting when considering landscape

Advanced work in schools and adult work

In the three-dimensional field some very interesting preliminary drawings for sculpture and modelling can be made using finger paint. As in a painting the basic lines are established and the similarities between a finger painting and a piece of work in clay become very apparent (figure 135). The isolation of a form, using a piece of card or a sponge, creates a very strong silhouette which can help the pupil to establish the shape of his sculpture or carving (see figure 135).

In the more academic study of art and art processes much valuable work can be done when studying the history of monoprinting. The similarity between this process and other print methods such as linocutting, screen printing and lithography should be emphasized, especially when establishing the basic concepts of reverse printing and multiple colour prints.

The print techniques of Rembrandt, William Blake, Lautrec, Gauguin, Matisse, Klee, Picasso, Ernst, Roualt and Dubuffet could all be studied, as many of their techniques can be used when producing monoprints from finger paint (figure 136). The work of Dubuffet is of particular interest as he was one of the first artists to assemble monoprint textures into collages, to create abstract designs.

135 Finger paint being used to establish the basic form of a clay figure. The similarities between finger painting and clay modelling are very apparent when working in this way

136 Monoprint *Clown with Monkey* by George Rouault. Examples like this help the older student to realize the potential of monotype printing, especially when considering figurative compositions
Collection, The Museum of Modern Art, New York

▶

137–8a Teachers using finger paint at an in-service art workshop. The value of this medium on courses is that the therapeutic aspect of finger painting helps to break down basic inhibitions about drawing and allows the teachers to produce large free drawings and prints

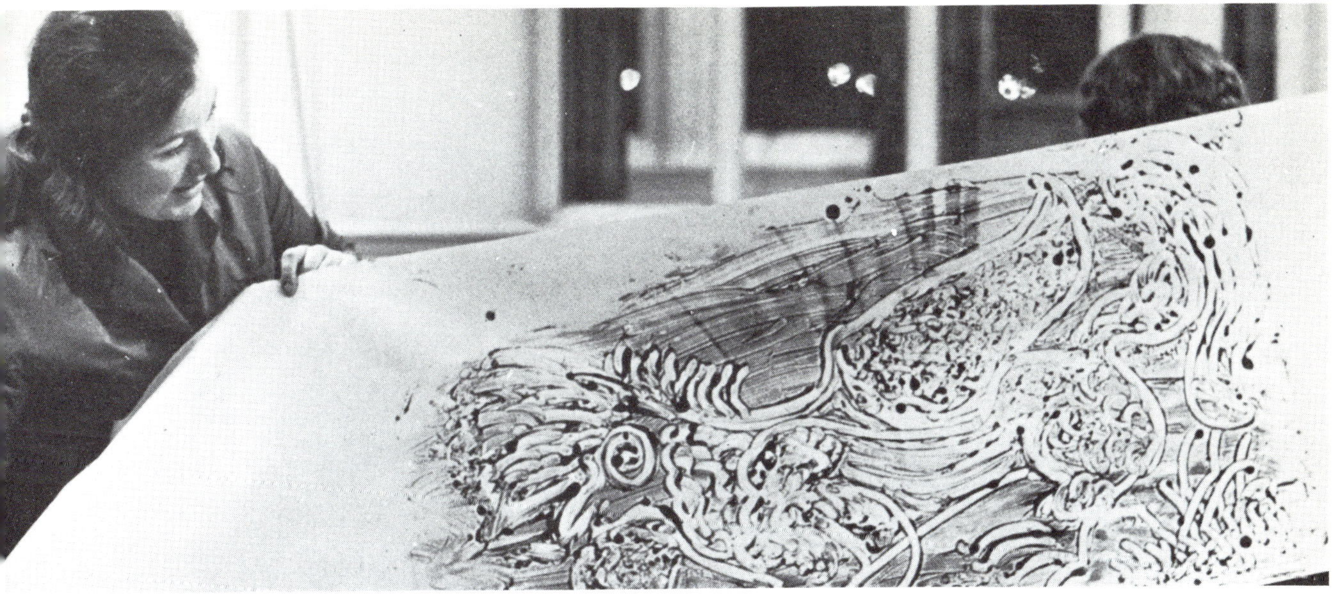

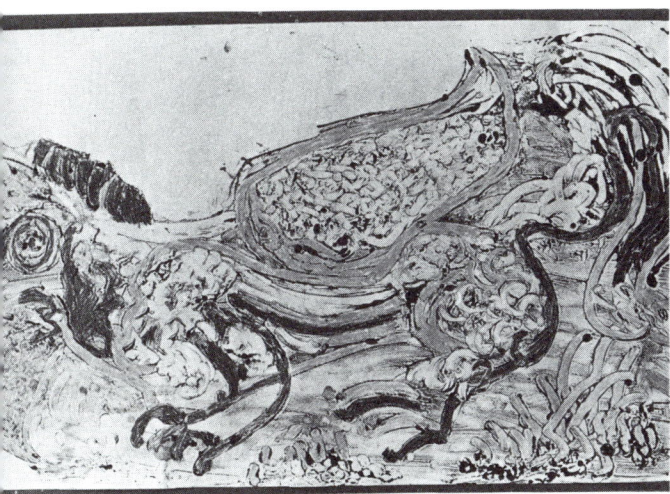

138b A development of the bird theme

138c Detail of bird collage

Finger painting
as therapy

Therapy for the physically handicapped

Painting activities for the physically handicapped are often consciously intended to stimulate certain muscular activities, to help co-ordination, and to develop a fuller use of the senses, especially touch. The finger painting activities described in this book cover a wide range of muscular movements, as can be seen in figures 139–42, and can easily be adapted by therapists to their particular needs.

Since the 1920s, when Ruth Shaw first developed the basic techniques of finger painting for educational purposes, it has also been closely associated with therapy, for both the mentally and the physically handicapped.

Teachers for the educationally sub-normal often find that particular children are capable of mental and artistic growth far beyond their abilities to express themselves with the written word. Finger painting may be used to stimulate this creativity and so help to build up a range of experiences which, in turn, can be the starting point for their other work.

Finger painting also allows the older child or the adult to regress into an infantile play experience. The painting can therefore be an accurate reflection of the artist's inner self and may be used for analysis, but this is a highly specialized technique and should be left to experts.

The main purpose of this type of work is obviously to

retrain the body, and the creative side is of less importance. However, through daily repetition of a given range of movements, linked with free play, co-ordination is likely to become more automatic and consequently the paintings will become more fluid.

As with any sort of occupational therapy, the benefit of finger painting is in the change of attitude of the patient. Finger paint – therapeutic by its very nature, like clay and sand – not only encourages physical development but also kindles enthusiasm, which is the basis of any cure.

Therapy in the classroom

The first years of a child's school life are often the most difficult, and *all* children require activities such as finger painting so that they can lose themselves and become completely absorbed into the new school situation. Finger painting is also particularly valuable in helping the difficult or problem child adapt to classroom life. The very sensitive child, for example, may be able to lose himself in this type of activity, and so become more self-confident and assured. On the other hand the extroverted child has an opportunity to rid himself of some of his surplus energy while he is physically involved with the painting activity.

Finger painting as an aid to development

As a general rule all finger painting must commence with a period of free exploration, no matter what the required end product. One can, however, consider four main areas of development, both in the normal and the handicapped child, where finger painting can be an aid.

Physical development: by finger painting a child will be able to explore large arm movements, as well as small, delicate finger movements; and as both hands are used equally, this helps the whole body to be involved and thus aids co-ordination and motor control. It is also an activity which affords enjoyment and success for the child with weak manual control, as the material can be moved easily.

Intellectual development: finger painting is a useful aid to colour recognition and language development ('This is a straight line', 'This is a red circle', etc), especially if the teacher and child work together, creating the situation ('Here is a man – now you draw his arms and legs').

Finger painting can also be used as a pre-writing activity. Left to right writing patterns can be practised leading to Marion Richardson patterns. These were originally developed to encourage children to write with a free rhythmic flow across the paper. The use of simple repeated letter forms can create many interesting designs in finger paint, especially if the negative shapes are emphasized when developing the prints. Likewise big free capitals cut into the finger paint with a piece of card and then printed can be the starting point for textile prints.

This type of work is especially important for the mentally handicapped child who often needs a lot of practice before he has the confidence to start writing.

Emotional development: finger painting gives the aggressive or very lively child a play activity where he can work off some of his surplus energy, and its 'instant success' can increase the self-confidence of the timid or nervous child. The ease with which the images he has created can be erased is also a valuable way in which a child's tension can be lessened.

Social development: many young children find difficulty in making social contact when they start school, and finger painting could be used to encourage them to work together – painting together in groups or printing backgrounds for friezes, which could then be developed into further group projects. Sharing activities helps people to share ideas.

139–42 Daniel demonstrates the wide range of body movements which can be achieved in finger painting. As all the fingers of both hands are active in this type of free play, it helps to establish motor-control and co-ordination. Curved lines, straight lines, thin lines and complicated lines can all be explored and used as an introduction to writing patterns Improvization should be encouraged and figures 141–2 show Daniel standing above the painting surface so that he can explore a completely new range of body movements

Conclusion

All the processes and projects described in this book can be accomplished using either homemade finger paints or the manufactured variety. In the past few years, however, artists have experimented with many other types of paint for finger painting, with varying degrees of success. In America artists have re-applied these techniques for use with oil paint, producing many interesting and highly textural paintings – but the difficulties of cleaning hands and surfaces obviously precludes this in schools. On the other hand the new range of acrylic polymers and synthetic resins, which have encouraged similar explorations, could easily be used by older pupils.

Although exploration and the use of a variety of materials is exciting, and a logical extension of the art form, it should never be forgotten that the spontaneity of finger painting, as related to the child's creative development, is the most important consideration.

◀ 143 *Rain Forest* by Sidney Nolan. In his work Nolan uses many of the processes and technique discussed in this book to achieve the particular surface qualities he requires in his paintings
By courtesy of the Cecil Higgins Art Gallery, Bedford

Further reading

The following books may be of interest as they are concerned with many of the points discussed in this book

Finger Painting, Ruth Shaw, Little Brown, New York
Pre-school and Infant Art, Kenneth Jameson, Studio Vista, London: Viking, New York
Children and Creative Activity, Daphne Plaskow, Society of Education Through Art, London
Introducing Surface Printing, Peter Green, Batsford, London: Watson-Guptill Publications, New York
Printmaking with Monotype, Henry Rasmusen, Chilton, New York
Exploring Finger Paint, Victoria Bedford Betts, Davies Publications, Worcester, Massachusetts
Finger Painting and Personality Diagnosis, P. F. Napoli, Journal Press, Provincetown, Massachusetts

Suppliers

Great Britain
Finger paints, finger painting paper and all artists' materials

E J Arnold Limited
Butterley Street
Leeds LS10 1AX

Binney and Smith (Europe) Limited
Ampthill Road
Bedford

A Brown and Sons Limited
Perth Street West
Hull
Yorkshire

John Dobbie
73 High Street
London SW17

Dryad
Northgates
Leicester

Educational Supply Association Limited
Pinnacles
Harlow ·
Essex

James France Toys Limited
10 Kensington Square
London N8 and
7 Gun Street
Reading
Berkshire

James Galt and Co Limited
Brookfield Road
Cheadle
Cheshire

B Garrad Limited
Water Lane
Kings Langley
Hertfordshire

Hamley Limited
200–202 Regent Street
London W1

Miller's Drawing Materials
54 Queens Street
Glasgow C1

Thomas Hope and Sankey Hudson Limited
Ashton Mill
Chapeltown Street
Manchester M1 2NH

Jarrold and Sons Limited
Cowgate
Norwich NOR 35A

Midland Educational Co Limited
583 Moseley Road
Birmingham 12

Reeves and Sons Limited
Lincoln Road
Enfield
Middlesex and branches

Sisson and Parker Limited
St Mark's Street
Nottingham

A Wheaton and Co Limited
143 Fore Street
Exeter
Devon

United States of America
Finger paints and finger painting paper

Binney and Smith Inc
Madison Avenue
New York

also from local artists' colormen